Jean Montagard and Chri

# DELICIOUS HOME-MADE
# PETITS FOURS

*English version by Sarah Joyce*

SEARCH PRESS

# DELICIOUS HOME-MADE PETITS FOURS

Petits fours are attractively decorated miniature cakes or fancy biscuits which always lend a note of delight and a 'touch of class' to a large buffet, a small reception, or to a tea party. Large cakes cut into slices, or traditionally sized 'patisseries' are not regarded as petits fours because they require a plate and a fork. Petits fours are for eating with your fingers. Making them, however, is fairly time-consuming too. Consequently they are expensive to buy, so that it is advantageous to be able to make them at home.

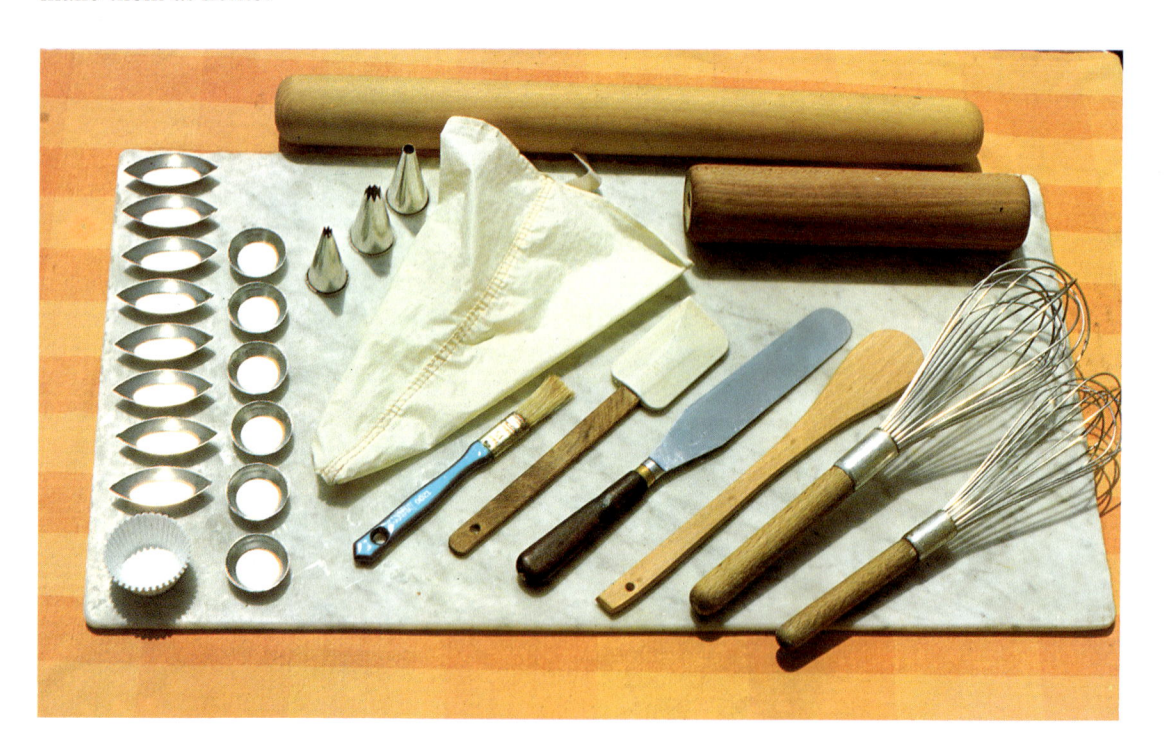

## Equipment *(see picture above)*
Several special, but inexpensive, tools are necessary, which are useful in all 'patisserie' making:
- a wooden rolling pin;
- a small rolling pin in either wood or metal (for nougatine);
- a smooth work surface (marble, metal or plastic);
- one or two balloon whisks;
- a wooden spatula, or scraper;
- a palette knife;
- a rubber or plastic scraper;
- a pastry brush;
- small round, and oval, moulds;
- a piping bag with a set of three nozzles (plain and rose pipes);
- small paper cases.

## Quantities

At a tea party one should allow about ten petits fours per person. At a savoury buffet, a small tea party, or as a dessert, four or five should be sufficient.

The quantities given in each recipe will produce about 12 cakes. It is obviously better to cook in batches and make, for example, all the choux pastry based cakes you need at the same time.

There are thirteen recipes offered in this book. The petits fours themselves may be made one or two days in advance and stored in airtight tins. If they are decorated with cream they will keep for one day in a refrigerator.

## Baking

Baking temperatures are given in degrees for modern ovens. For thermostat controlled ovens the equivalents are:
50°C=122°F   100°C=212°F   150°C=302°F
180°C=356°F

*Different uses of choux pastry*

## Ready-made products

These can be bought in large supermarkets, specialist grocers or delicatessens:
- dried baker's yeast;
- tinned or powdered praliné;
- coffee essence;
- vanilla essence;
- fondant (for icing);
- apricot glaze;
- chocolate vermicelli, coffee beans (for decoration).

Note that the petits fours given here only use natural ingredients, with the exception of colouring. Brown sugar is preferable to white for its dietary quality and because it gives a better colour.

## Pastries and cream

The basic shortbread style biscuit mixture, and choux pastry, both serve as a base for several different kinds of petits fours. The quantities given will allow you to make at least twelve cakes of each variety but the amount will vary. The same goes for the trimmings: butter cream, pastry cream, almond cream, or chocolate ganache (see page 15).

# GENOESE CAKE

This is easy to make. Afterwards it is cut into small pieces and stuffed and coated with coffee butter cream (mocha) or with chocolate cream.

4 eggs
125 g (5 oz.) sugar
125 g (5 oz.) flour

These quantities will give 24 petits fours. It is difficult to divide the ingredients in two and still obtain a successful sponge. Therefore if you only need 12 cakes keep half the sponge for another occasion.

Blend the eggs and sugar together in a bowl. Heat over a bain-marie (Picture 1) or double-saucepan and whisk for 5 or 6 minutes (2), or 2 or 3 minutes with an electric beater. When lifted on the whisk a little of the mixture should fall back and form a sort of ribbon on the remaining mixture in the bowl (3). Remove from the heat and continue whisking until the mixture is cool. Then sift the flour through a fine sieve and gently fold in (4). Mix well but do not beat (5). Pour the mixture into a greased and floured mould. Bake for 20–25 minutes in an oven pre-heated to 150°C (302°F). Leave to cool (6). Turn out.

# BUTTER CREAM

4 egg yolks
125 g (5 oz.) castor sugar
150 g (6 oz.) butter

Begin by making a syrup that will pour easily: put the sugar and some water (about 3 tblsp) in a pan. Bring to the boil and simmer for about 4 minutes (Picture 1).

To check whether the sugar has cooked, dip your fingers in cold water (2), and quickly pick up a little of the syrup (3): there is no risk of getting scalded. Dip your fingers in the water again; the syrup should form a small, soft ball.

Remove the syrup from the heat and very gently pour it over the egg yolks (4), and whisk continuously for about 5 minutes (5). When the mixture is cold, add the softened butter, and continue beating to a smooth consistency (6).

Flavour the cream with an essence of your choice.

# MOCHAS

Genoese sponge (page 4)
Coffee butter cream (page 5)
50 g (2 oz.) flaked and toasted almonds

*Syrup*
1 decilitre (3 fl. oz.) water
50 g (2 oz.) sugar
lemon rind
1 vanilla pod

First prepare the syrup; put the ingredients in a pan, bring to the boil, then remove from the heat.

Cut the Genoese cake in two, slicing through its thickness (Picture 1). Brush on the syrup (2), then spread on a layer of butter cream (3). Form the cake into a sandwich and leave it in the refrigerator for about 30 minutes.

Brown the almonds in the oven or under a grill; but keep your eye on them.

Take the cake out of the refrigerator, trim away the rounded edges, and cut into 12 equal portions (4).

Spread each portion, on all its sides, with butter cream (5). Dip the sides into the almonds (6) or crushed nougatine (see page 30). Decorate with butter cream, using a piping bag and rose nozzle (7).

7

*Mochas may also be decorated with heavier dots in, for example, domino patterns.*

# BASIC BISCUIT MIXTURE

1

This shortbread pastry serves as a base for several different types of petits fours: such as Lunettes, Tartlets and Polkas.

125 g (5 oz.) plain flour
65 g (2½ oz.) softened butter
50 g (2 oz.) sugar
1 egg yolk
Pinch of salt

2

Make a well with the flour and place all the other ingredients in the centre (Picture 1).

Blend the ingredients, starting in the centre and working outwards (2). Work the pastry by kneading it with your hands (3) and then stretching it with your palms (4). Roll it into a ball, and put it in the refrigerator to rest and firm up.

3

4

# LUNETTES

Basic biscuit mixture (page 8)
2 tablespoons blackcurrant or raspberry jam
icing sugar

Roll the biscuit mixture until it is about 6mm(¼ in.) thick. Using a small cutter, cut out 24 small rounds (Picture 1). With a palette knife place them on an ungreased baking sheet (2). On half the rounds cut 3 holes with the tip of a plain nozzle (3).

Bake for 14 minutes in an oven pre-heated to 180°C (356°F).

*Decoration.* Dust the cut-out halves with icing sugar (4). Spread a little jam on the plain halves (5), and sandwich the two halves together (6).

# ALMOND CREAM

40 g (1¾ oz.) ground almonds
40 g (1¾ oz.) icing sugar
80 g (3½ oz.) butter
1 egg
1 tablespoon plain flour

The mixture of ground almonds and icing sugar can be bought ready-made but it is very easy to make for yourself. In a small bowl whisk the ground almonds and icing sugar together with the softened butter. Add the egg (Picture 1), then the flour, and beat to a smooth consistency (2).

# STRAWBERRY TARTLETS

Basic biscuit mixture (page 8)
Almond cream (page 10)
20 strawberries
2 tablespoons melted apricot glaze

5

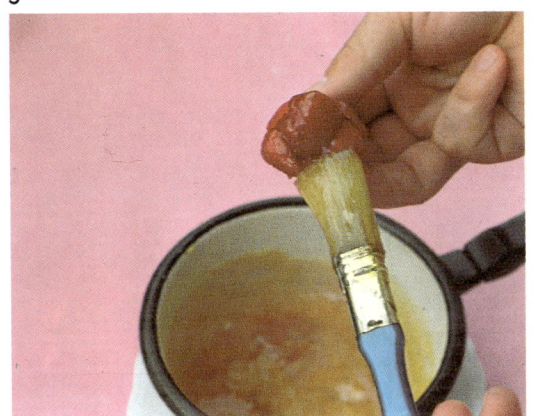

*Assembling the tartlets.* Fill ungreased round moulds with the biscuit mixture which has been rolled to a thickness of 6mm (¼ in.). Next, fill these with almond cream and bake them together with the other tartlets in an oven pre-heated to 180°C (356°F) for 20–25 minutes. Turn out and leave to cool. Remove the stalks from the strawberries and wipe them (do not wash). Cut and press them into the tartlets (3, 4). Spread the apricot glaze over them, and leave (5).

These tartlets may also be made with pieces of fresh fruit (pineapple, raspberries) or tinned fruit such as peach, apricot or pear.

# WALNUT TARTLETS

1 
2 
3 
4 
5

# Walnut tartlets

## Walnut cream
40 g (1¾ oz.) walnuts
40 g (1¾ oz.) icing sugar
40 g (1¾ oz.) butter
1 egg
1 tablespoon plain flour

## Tartlets
Basic biscuit mixture (page 8)
Walnut cream (above)
12 green walnuts
2 tablespoons melted apricot glaze

Walnut cream is made in exactly the same way as almond cream (page 10). Replace the almonds with the same amount of ground walnuts (Pictures 1, 2).

Roll the biscuit mixture until it is 6mm (¼ in.) thick. Turn into ungreased round moulds (3) and then fill them with walnut cream (4). Bake together with other tartlets in an oven pre-heated to 180°C (356°F) for 20–25 minutes. Turn out and leave to cool.

Place a green walnut on each tartlet and glaze quickly (5).

# GANACHE TARTLETS

# Ganache tartlets

*Ganache, or canache, is a basic mixture of chocolate and double cream. It is used for decoration and also to flavour creams and fondants.*

## Ganache
250 g (10 oz.) eating chocolate
⅛ litre (¼ pint) milk
25 g (1 oz.) butter
1 tablespoon unsweetened cocoa

## Tartlets
Basic biscuit mixture (page 8)
Almond cream (page 10)
Ganache
Chocolate vermicelli

Melt the chocolate in the milk over a bain-marie or double-saucepan (Picture 1), stirring continuously. When the cream is smooth, remove from the heat. Add the butter and continue stirring (2). Leave the ganache to cool – its consistency should be a thick smooth paste.

*Assembling the tartlets.* Roll the biscuit mixture until about 6mm (¼ in.) thick (3), and turn into ungreased oval moulds (the mixture itself contains sufficient fat). Fill each tartlet with almond cream (4). Bake for 20–25 minutes in an oven pre-heated to 180°C (356°F). Turn out immediately, and leave to cool.

Decorate the tartlets with ganache, using a small rose nozzle (5). Dip the tips of each tartlet in the chocolate vermicelli (6).

# CHOUX PASTRY

¼ litre (½ pint) water
100 g (4 oz.) butter
Pinch of salt
Pinch of sugar
150 g (6 oz.) flour
5 eggs

*This serves as a base for many of the petits fours given in the following pages: coffee and lemon choux cakes, chocolate éclairs, and Swans. A strip of choux pastry is also used on the Polkas.*

Put the water, salt, sugar and butter in a pan over a lively flame. Bring to the boil (Picture 1) and lower the heat. Pour in all the flour (2) and beat vigorously with a wooden spatula or spoon (3). Increase the heat and continue beating for about 1 minute: the mixture should dry slightly and detach itself from the sides of the pan (4). *The success of this pastry relies on energetic beating while over the heat*. Remove from the heat. One by one, add the eggs and beat continuously to a smooth consistency (5, 6).

*Baking*. Brush some melted butter over a baking sheet (7). Fill a piping bag fitted with a fairly wide rose nozzle (8). Pipe out the pastry (9). Mix an egg yolk and a tablespoonful of water and brush this over the cakes (10). You could bake different shapes of choux on the same tray (11). The choux cakes should be golden and remain firm when pressed. Remove from the tray and leave to cool. It is advisable to pierce a hole through the side of the cakes to allow the steam to escape.

10

11

# CRÈME PÂTISSIÈRE *(Confectioner's custard)*

*All choux cakes are filled with this cream, flavoured with the essences of your choice.*

½ litre (1 pint) milk
125 g (5 oz.) sugar
4 egg yolks
55 g (2 oz.) flour

Put the milk on to boil. Meanwhile, in another pan, mix the egg yolks and sugar (Picture 1). Still stirring, add the flour (2). Stir until you have a smooth cream (3). Pour in the boiling milk, a little at a time, stirring continuously (4). Replace the cream over a medium heat and let it cook for a minute or two while you continue stirring: it should thicken, but never let it boil, otherwise it will curdle (5). Then pour it quickly into a cold receptacle (6).

Leave to cool, but stir it from time to time to prevent a skin forming.

# SMALL COFFEE CHOUX CAKES

Choux pastry (pages 16–17)
Coffee-flavoured crème pâtissière – see opposite page
Coffee fondant
Coffee beans (soaked in liqueur or chocolate)

Flavour the crème pâtissière with a half teaspoonful of coffee essence.

With the point of a plain nozzle, punch a hole in each little choux cake (Picture 1). Then fill a piping bag with the crème pâtissière and pipe a blob into each hole in the cakes (2).

Flavour the fondant. Put it in a small double-saucepan and heat gently. Dip the choux cakes into the fondant (3) and place two coffee beans on each.

# SMALL LEMON CHOUX CAKES

Choux pastry (pages 16–17)
Lemon flavoured crème pâtissière (page 18)
Fondant
Lemon rind

Follow the same process as for the coffee choux cakes. Finely grate some lemon rind, plunge it into boiling water and remove immediately. Dip the choux cakes in the fondant and put a few pieces of rind on top of each.
*Note.* To obtain a lemon-flavoured cream, boil the lemon peel in the milk at the outset.

# CHOCOLATE ÉCLAIRS

Choux pastry (pages 16–17)
Chocolate crème pâtissière (page 18)
Chocolate fondant
Chocolate butter cream for decoration

Pipe the choux pastry in the shape of small logs, and bake at the same time as the other cakes. Flavour the cream ($1/3$ ganache, $2/3$ cream) and whisk. Garnish the éclairs following the same process as for the choux cakes. Flavour the fondant with a little ganache and dip the top of the éclairs in the mixture.

To decorate, make a small piping bag from some grease-proof paper. Pipe patterns of butter cream on to the éclairs. (See page 21, top picture.)

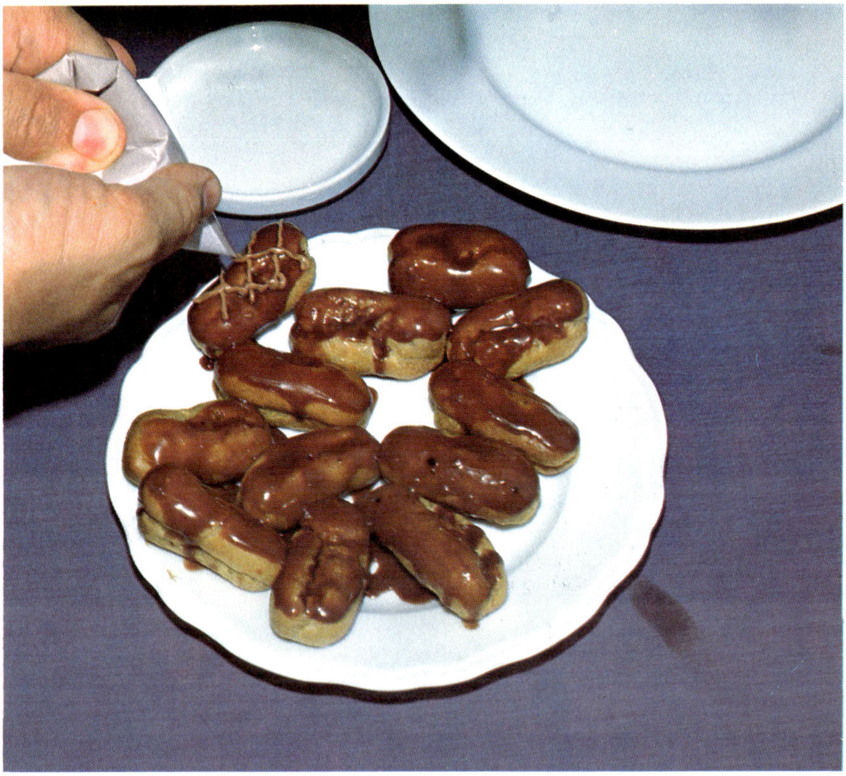

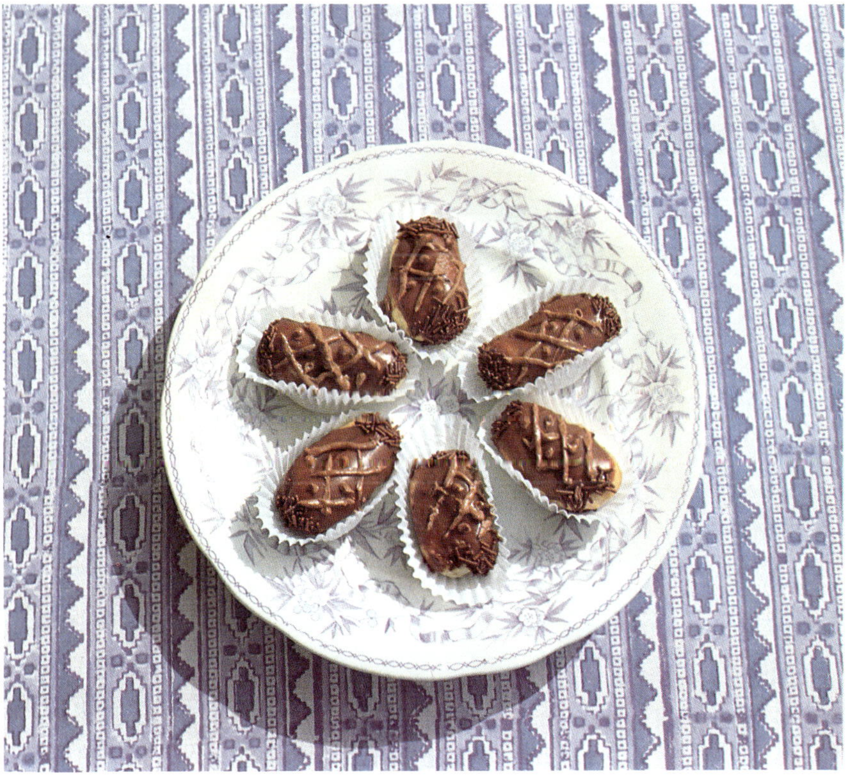

# SWANS

Choux pastry (pages 16–17)
1 egg yolk *and* 1 tablespoon water (to glaze)
**Chantilly**: 10 centilitres (⅕ pint) cream
25 g (1 oz.) icing sugar

This famous petit four is particularly spectacular. Practise your skill at keeping your hands steady as you pipe!

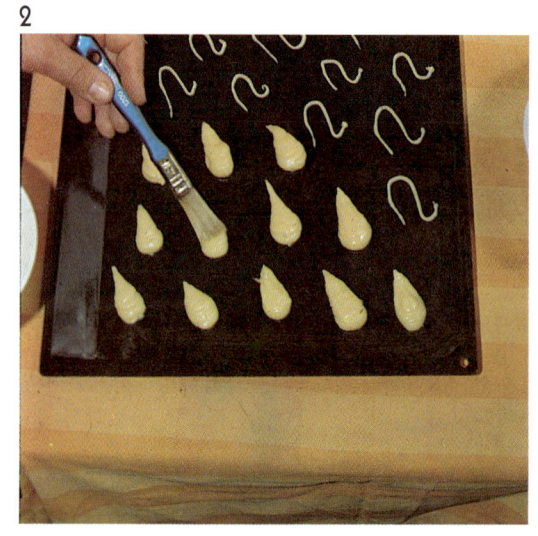

1

2

3

4

Using a piping bag with a plain nozzle, pipe the swans' bodies on to a greased baking sheet. With a small bag made from greaseproof paper pipe the swans' necks in 'S' shapes (Picture 1). (Make more than you will need as one or two will probably break.) Glaze them (2). Both shapes can be baked on the same tray although the bodies will take 20 minutes and the necks only 10 minutes in an oven preheated to 180°C (356°F). Watch them carefully.

Make the Chantilly by beating the cream with a whisk until it is stiff, then fold in the icing sugar.

*To assemble.* Cut off the top of the swan's body like a lid (3). This piece, cut into two, will make the wings. Pipe the Chantilly on to the bases (4) and press in the wings and necks (5). Dust with icing sugar.

# POLKAS

Basic biscuit mixture (page 8)
Choux pastry (pages 16–17)
Vanilla crème pâtissière (page 18)
1 egg yolk *and* 1 tablespoon water (to glaze)
icing sugar, for dusting

1

2

3

4

Roll the biscuit mixture until it is about 6mm (¼ in.) thick. Cut out rounds, and place on an ungreased baking tray. Glaze. Using a piping bag with a plain nozzle, pipe a strip of choux pastry around the edge (Picture 1). Glaze this strip (the first glazing should help the choux pastry to stick). Bake for 20 minutes in an oven pre-heated to 180°C (356°F). Remove, and leave to cool.

Pipe the crème pâtissière into the polkas (2). Dust with icing sugar (3) and make a caramelized pattern by placing a red-hot strip of metal (or skewer) on the sugar (4).

# ALMOND PRALINÉ MERINGUES

2 egg whites
60 g (2¼ oz.) sugar
praliné butter cream
50 g (2 oz.) flaked and toasted almonds

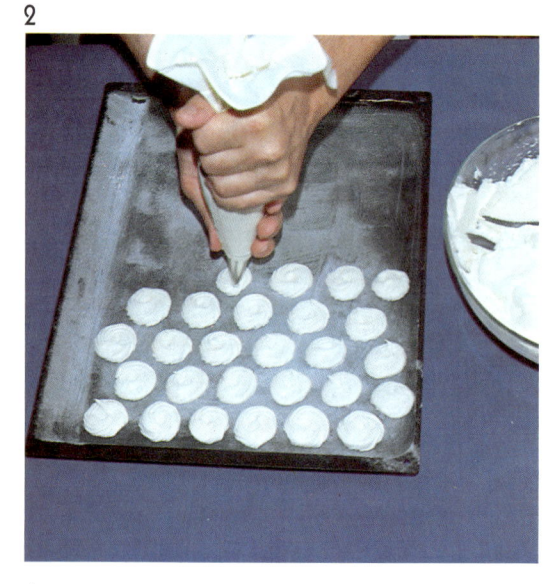

1

2

3

4

Each petit four is made with two meringues, with a layer of butter cream in between. You should be able to make at least 24 meringues.

Beat the egg whites with an electric beater until they are stiff. Slowly fold in the sugar, then continue to beat until the mixture is smooth and shiny (Picture 1). Using a piping bag with a rose nozzle, pipe the meringues on to a greased and floured baking tray (2). Bake for 30 minutes in an oven pre-heated to 100°C (212°F), and then for 1½–2 hours at 50°C (122°F). The meringues should not change colour.

Flavour the cream with powdered praliné and whisk it in.

Put a little cream on the peaked side of a meringue (3) and carefully press a second meringue against it. Spread butter cream in a ring around it, and roll in the flaked almonds or ground nougatine (page 30).

Place three almond flakes on top, held together with a little butter cream. With a rose nozzle, pipe a little cream around the edges.

1

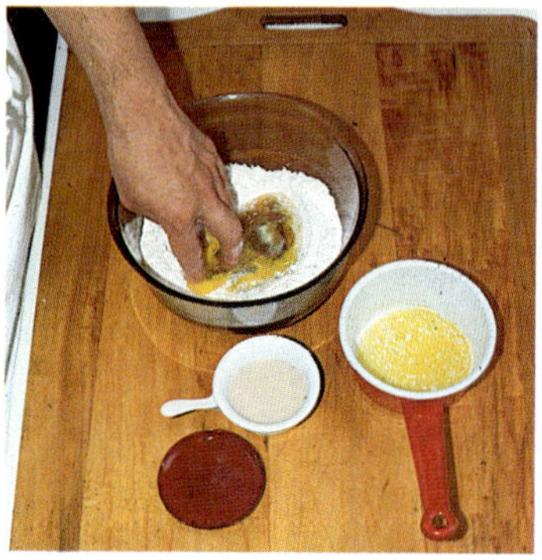

2

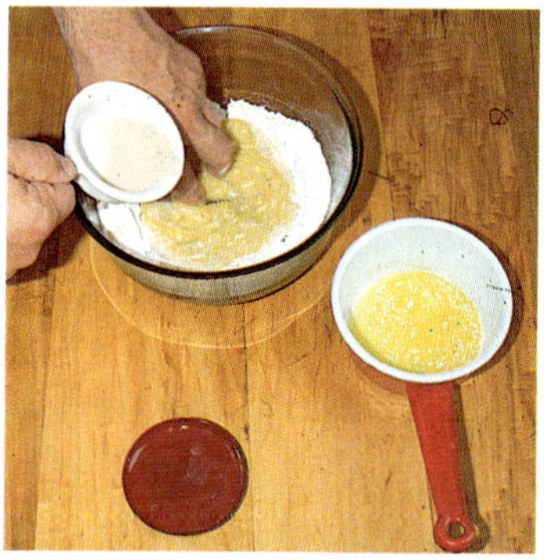

3

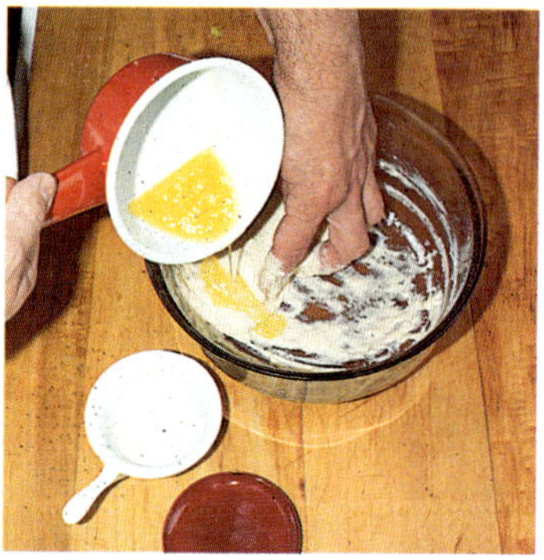

4

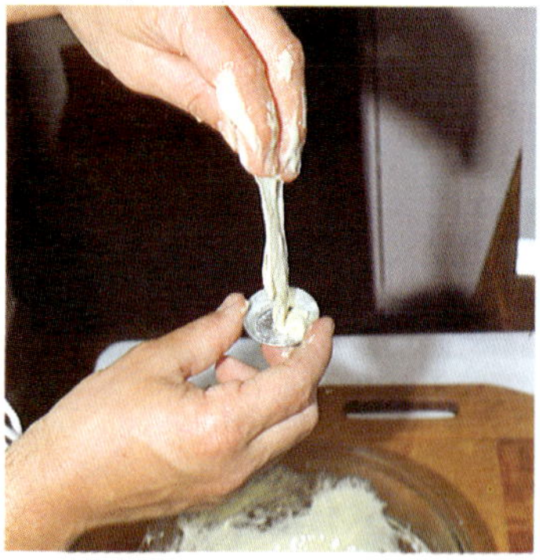

5

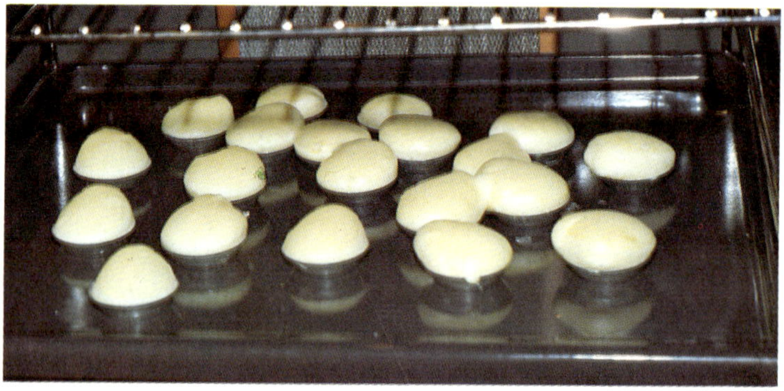

6

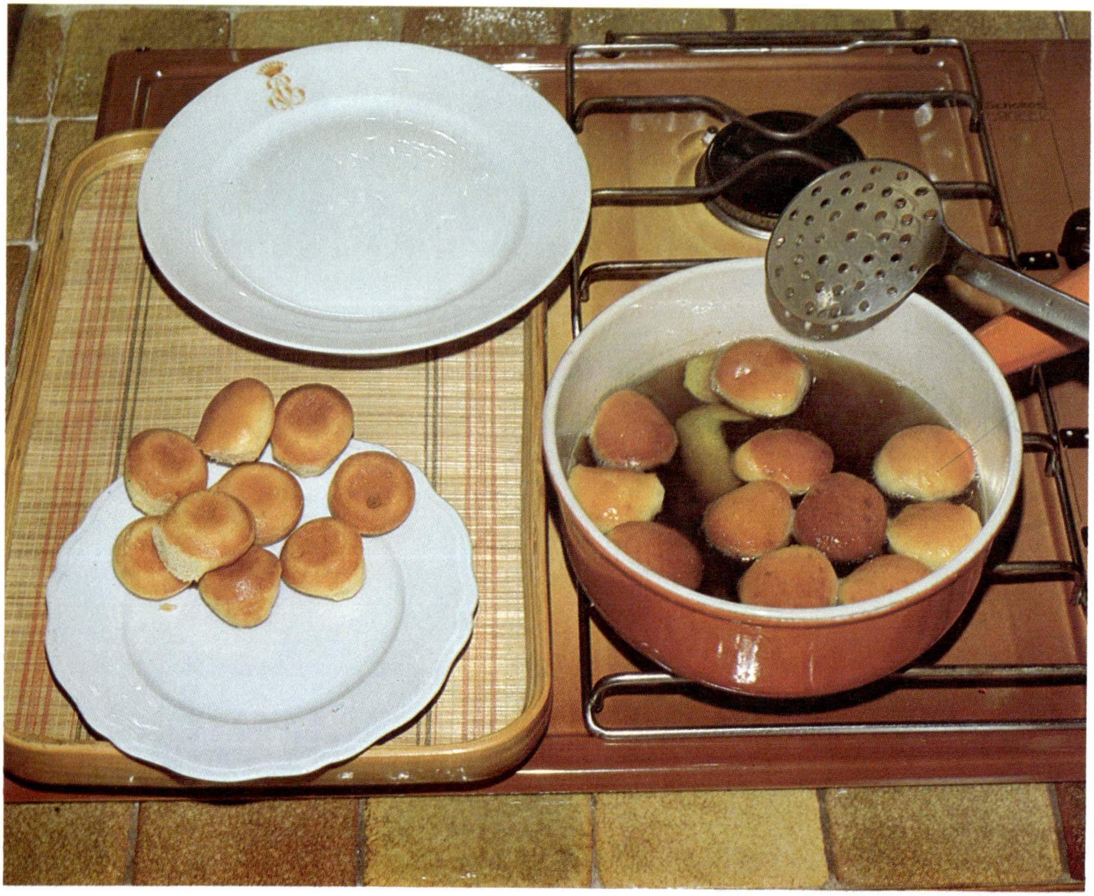

# CHANTILLY SPONGE-CAKES, OR BABAS

1 level teaspoon bakers' yeast
2 tablespoons warm water
80 g (3¼ oz.) plain flour
8 g (¼ oz.) sugar
Pinch of salt
25 g (1 oz.) butter (softened)
1 egg, beaten

It is difficult to make these quantities any less; however this recipe will produce about 20 cakes. Dissolve the yeast in the warm water, breaking it up in your fingers. Mix together in a large bowl the flour, salt, sugar and 1 egg (Picture 1). Add the yeast (2). Stir and fold in the melted butter (3). Pour the mixture into small, round, greased moulds (brushed with melted butter), so that the moulds are half-filled (4).

Leave the mixture to rise for about an hour at a temperature of 40°C (104°F) in the compartment either above or below the oven. It should double in size (5). Bake for 20 minutes at 180°C (356°F). Turn out immediately on to a wire rack and leave to cool.

*Syrup.* ½ litre water
250 g (7 oz.) sugar
Orange rind, finely grated
Lemon rind, finely grated
Vanilla pod

## Syrup and dipping

Put all the ingredients in a large pan, bring slowly to the boil, and remove from heat.

The part of each cake which was in the mould should be both more smooth and more porous: this is the part which will be decorated, and also dipped first.

Soak the sponge cakes in the pan of syrup (6) for 5 minutes, turn over, and leave for another 5 minutes. Drain the cakes and leave them on a plate (7).

Flavour them with a drop or two of rum or Kirsch, and put them into small paper cases. Decorate with left-over cream from the swans, and a raisin (8).

# NOUGATINE CONES

150 g (6 oz.) sugar
Lemon juice
80 g (3¼ oz.) flaked almonds
Coffee, or praliné,
butter cream

Nougatine is delicious, and easy to make provided that you work fast. It should be spread on a well-greased slab using a well-greased rolling pin – the greasing should be done before you start. Put the sugar and lemon juice in a pan over a gentle flame and stir continuously with a spatula (Picture 1). The sugar should melt and darken. Throw in the almonds (2) and stir for another 1–2 minutes. Stop stirring as soon as the whole mixture becomes darker (3).

Put the nougatine on a work slab and roll it (4). Cut out three rounds, using a ramekin as a guide (5). Divide each round into four. Using your fingers, form a cone with each piece (6, 7, 8).

**Warning**. You must work quickly, otherwise the nougatine will harden and become brittle. To soften it, put in in the oven for a few minutes at 100°C (212°F). Break and grind the remaining pieces (9) as they can replace the almonds to decorate other petits fours. Pipe butter cream to fill the cones.

# INDEX TO SUBJECTS AND RECIPES

Almond cream, 10
Almond praliné meringues, 26–7
Baking, 3
Basic biscuit mixture, 8
Butter cream, 5
Chantilly sponge cakes, or babas, 28–9
Chocolate éclairs, 20
Choux cakes, 19, 20
Choux pastry, 16–17
Coffee choux cakes, 19
Crème pâtissière, 18
Equipment, 2
Ganache tartlets, 14–15

Genoese cake, 4
Lemon choux cakes, 20
Lunettes, 9
Mochas, 6–7
Nougatine cones, 30–1
Pastries and cream, 3
Polkas, 24–5
Quantities, 3
Ready-made products, 3
Strawberry tartlets, 11
Swans, 22–3
Tartlets, 10–13
Walnut tartlets, 12–13

**EQUIVALENT TEMPERATURES**
TO CONVERT CENTIGRADE (°C) INTO FAHRENHEIT (°F) multiply by 9, divide by 5, and add 32.

TO CONVERT FAHRENHEIT (°F) TO CENTIGRADE (°C) subtract 32, multiply by 5, divide by 9.

First published in Great Britain 1986
by Search Press Ltd
Wellwood, North Farm Road,
Tunbridge Wells, Kent TN2 3DR

Originally published in France 1983
Copyright © Dessain et Tolra, Paris, 1983
English version Copyright © Search Press Ltd 1986

No part of this book, text or illustration, may be reproduced or transmitted in any form or by any means by print, photoprint, microfilm, photocopies, or in any way, known or as yet unknown, or stored in a retrieval system, without written permission obtained beforehand from Search Press.

Printed in Belgium by

ISBN 0 85532 582 8